Pierre-Auguste Renoir

Paintings

Informative edition

Based on Paintings of
Pierre-Auguste Renoir (1841-1919)
Presented by the european journalist
Iacob Adrian

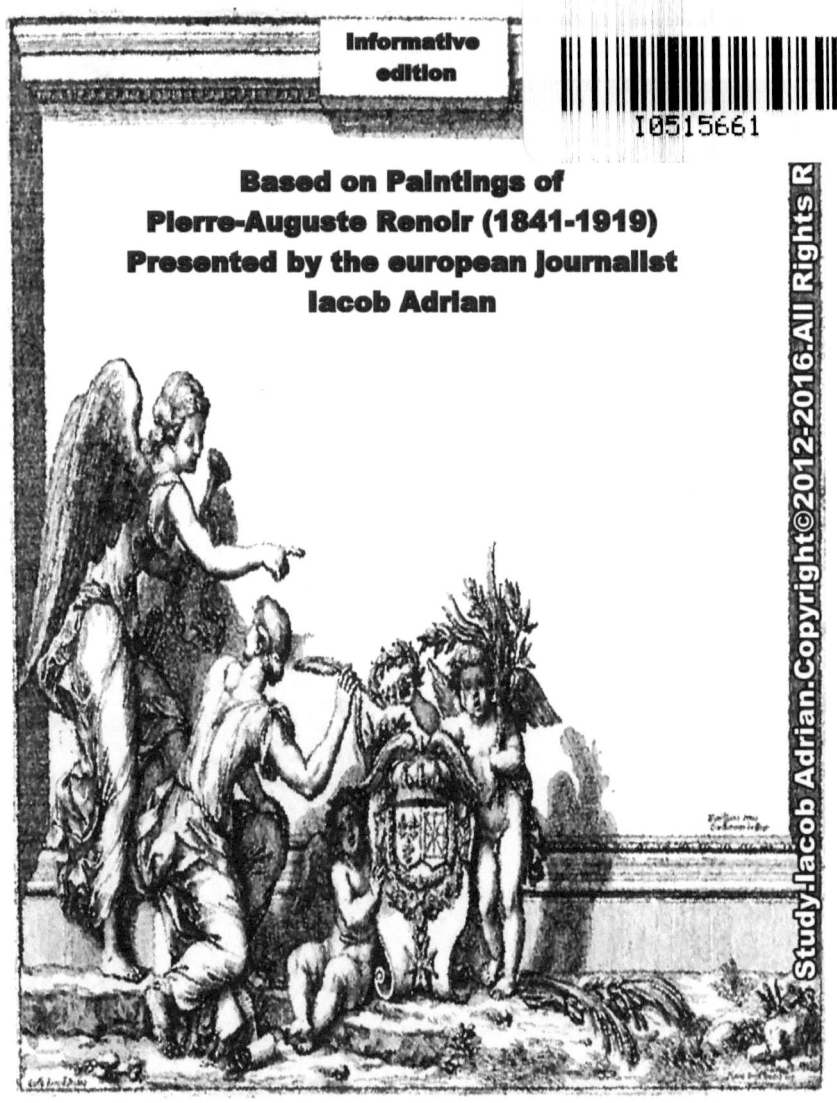

ISBN-13 : 978-1974589708 -- ISBN-10 : 1974589706

Notice

This documentary study use historic, archived documents. Because of this, some pages may look blurry or low quality. Still are included in this book because they have high value from critical, documentary, historical, informative and journalistic point of view.

Dtp and visual art
Iacob Adrian

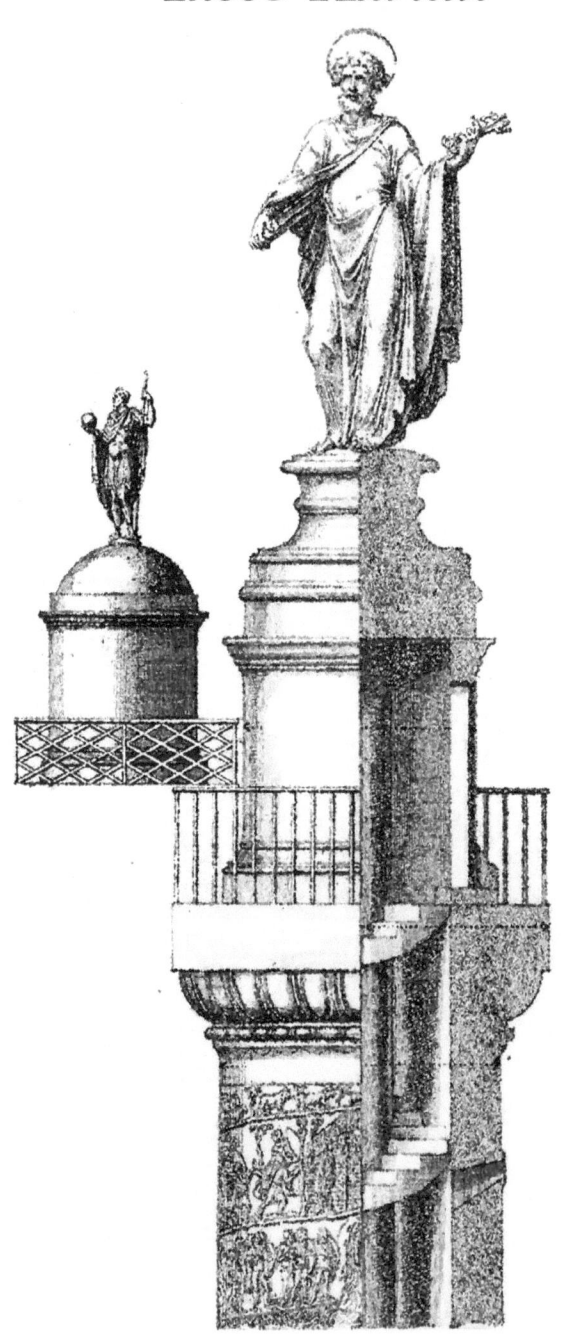

Editor
Iacob Adrian

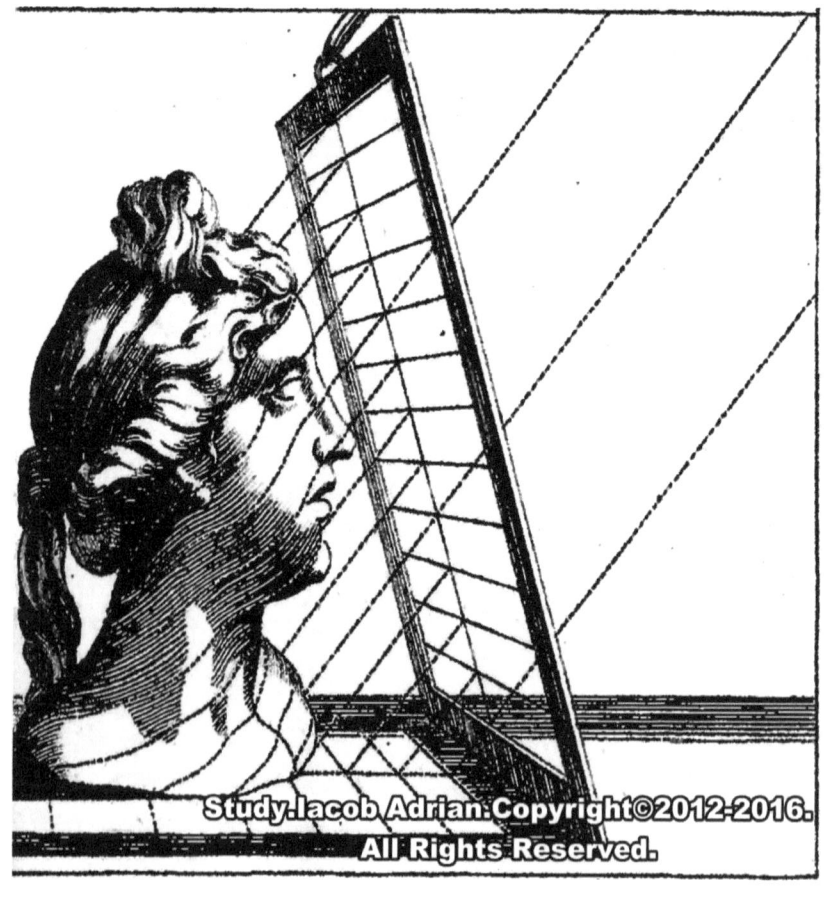

Editor statement

This is a series of classic books from classical authors.

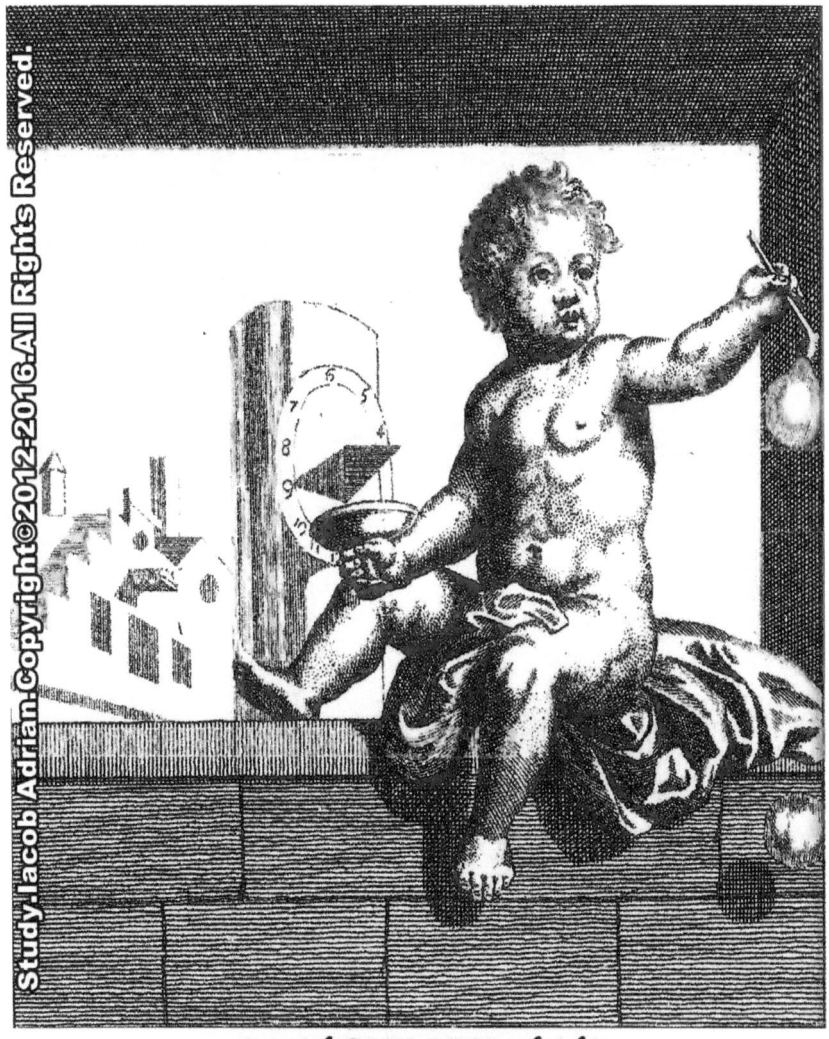

Copyright©2012-2016 Iacob Adrian
All Rights Reserved.

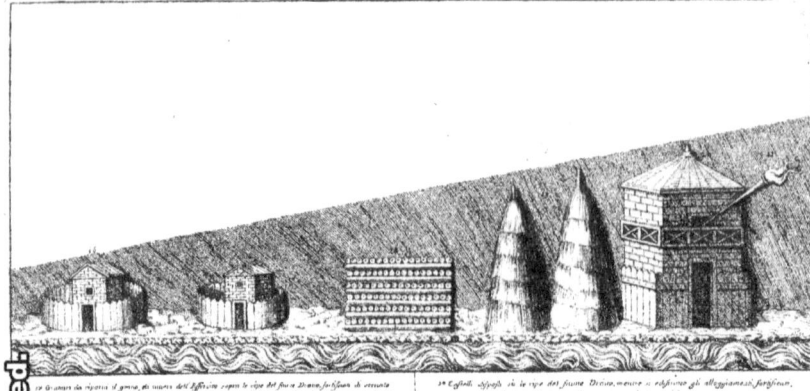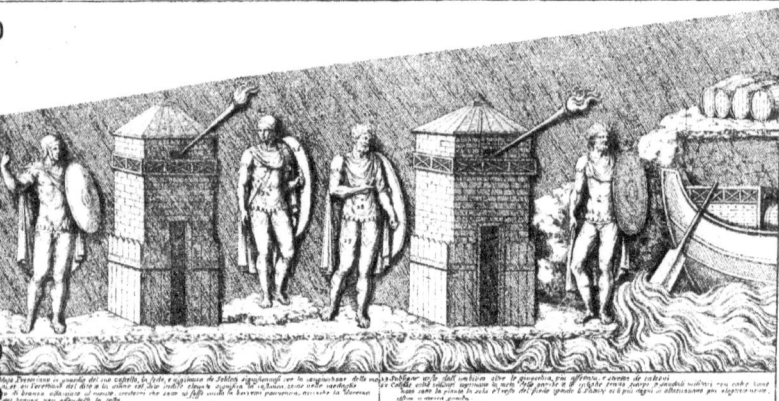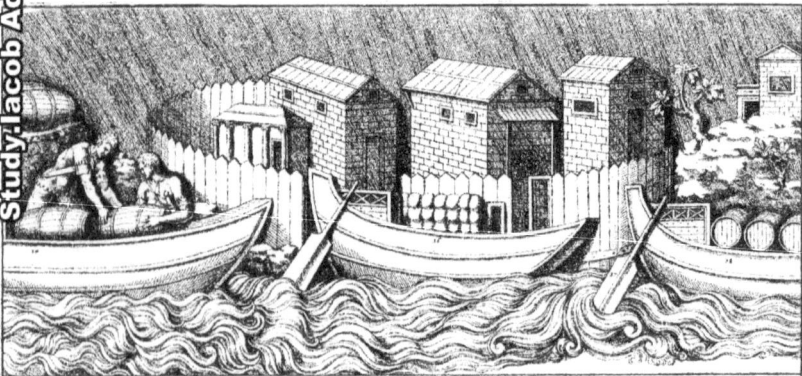

This little Book conveys the greetings of

....

to

....

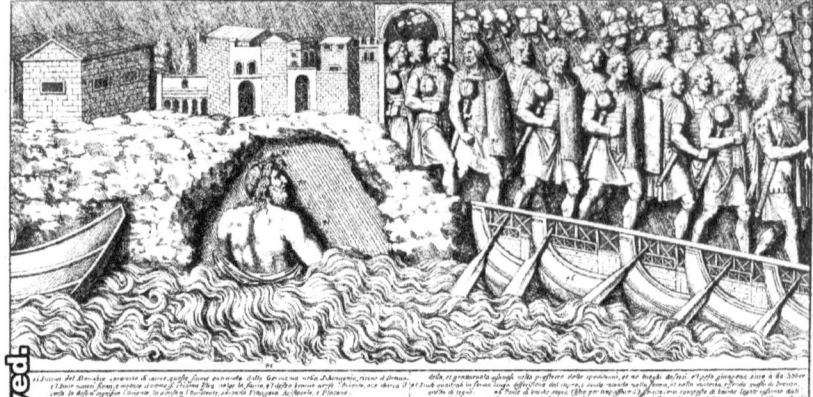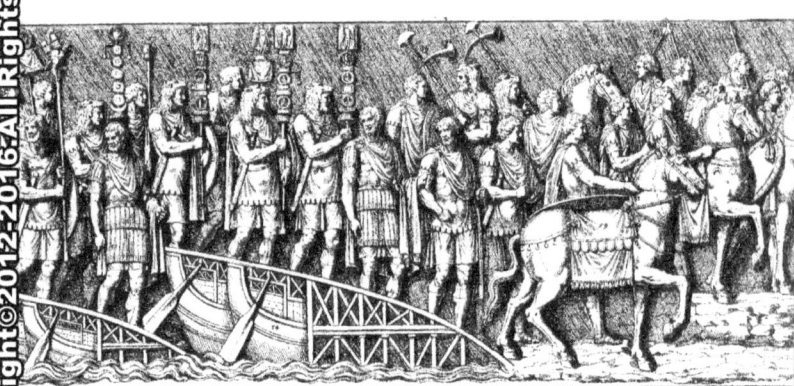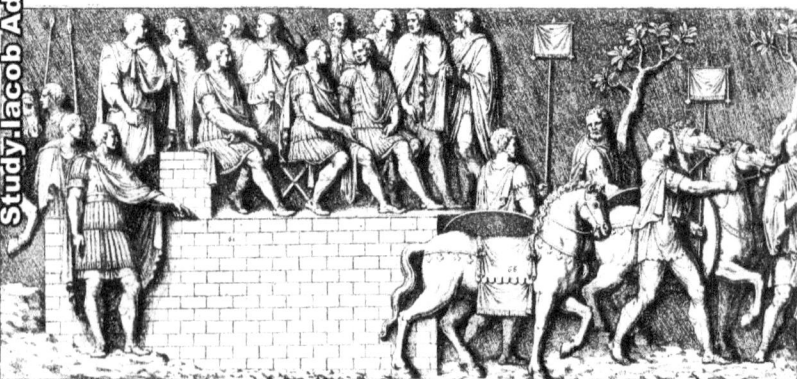

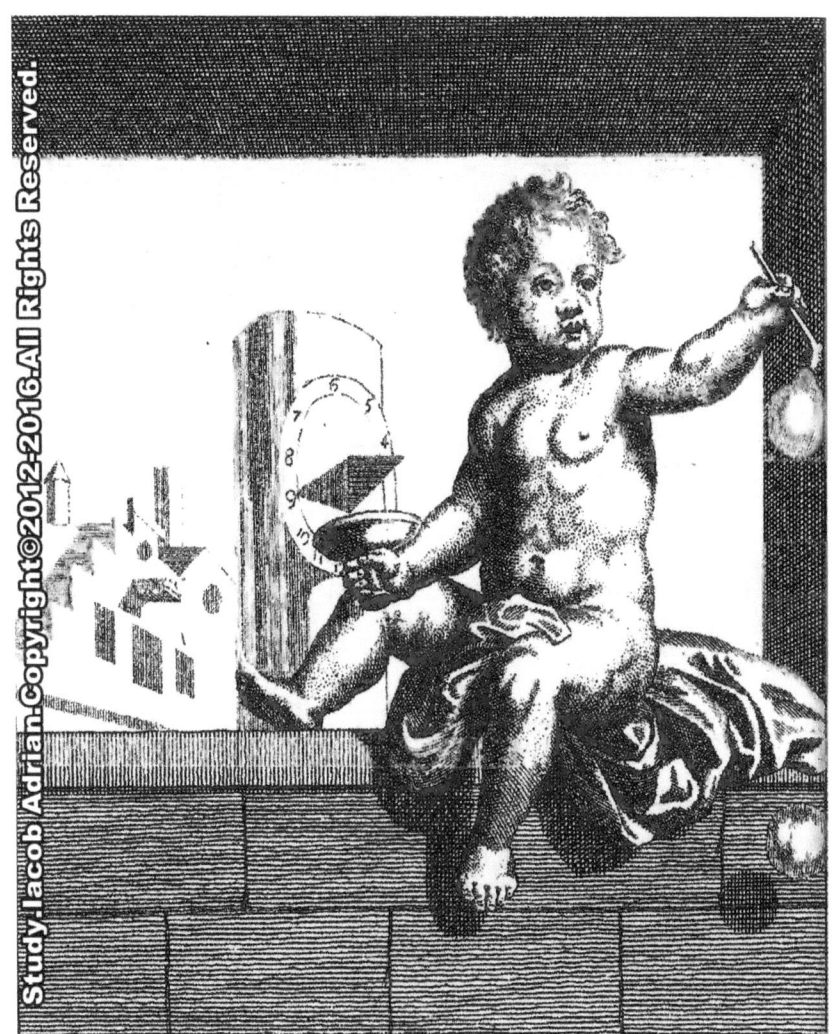

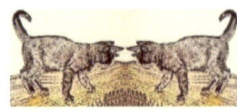

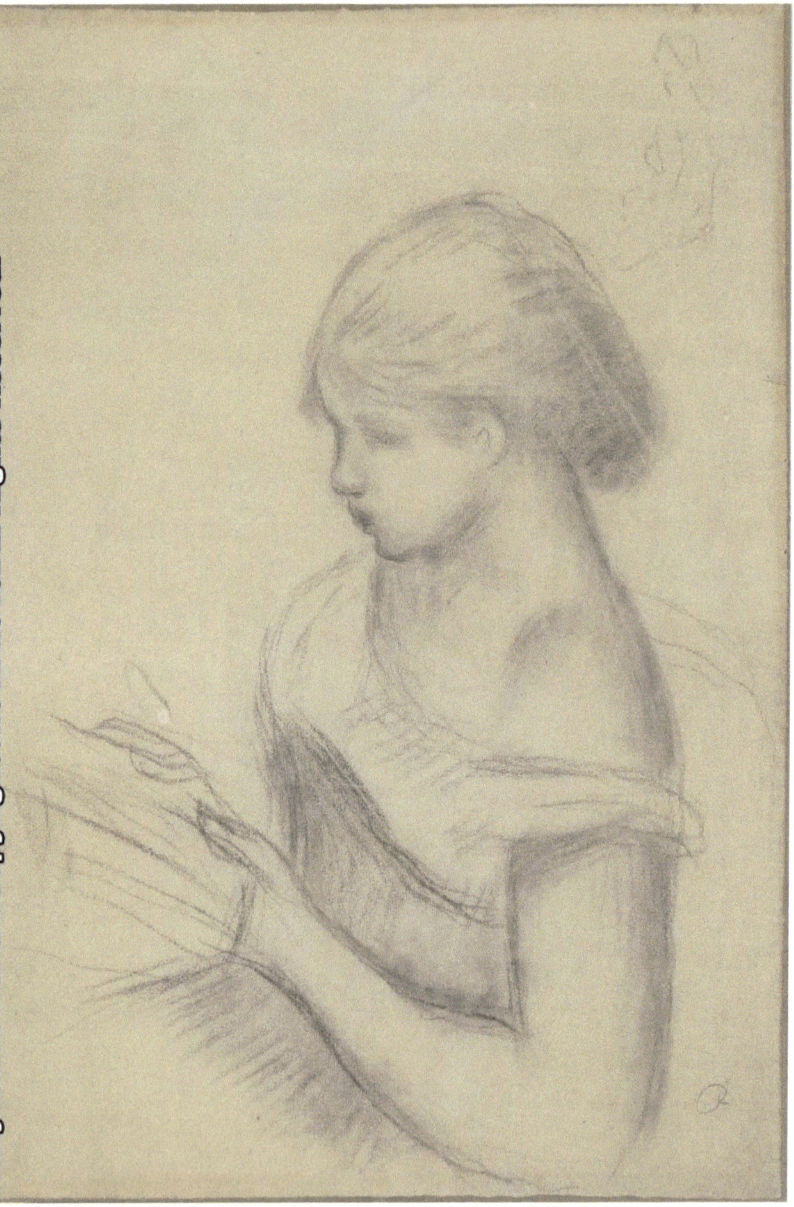

A Girl Reading (with a Sketch of Seated Woman)
Date : n.d.

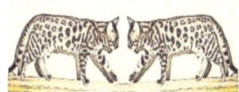

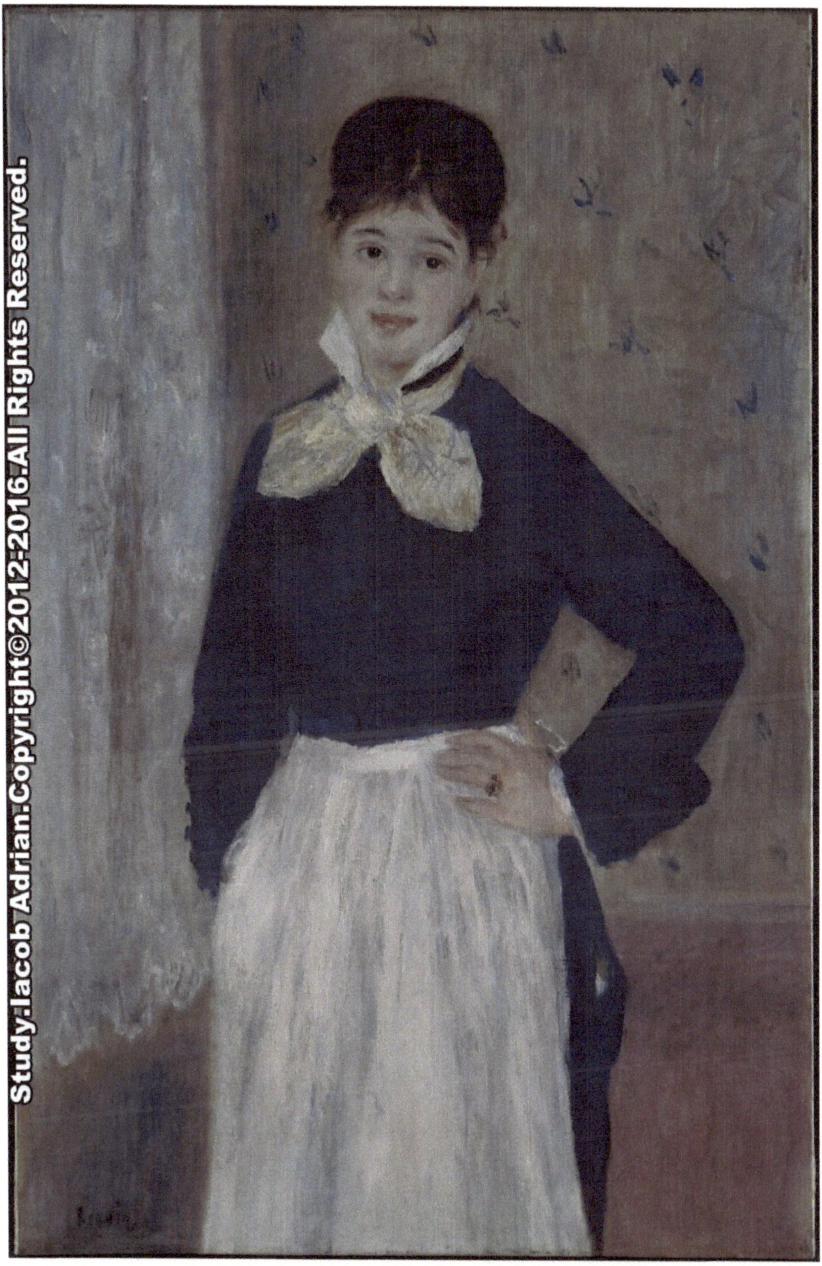

A Waitress at Duval's Restaurant
Date : circa 1875

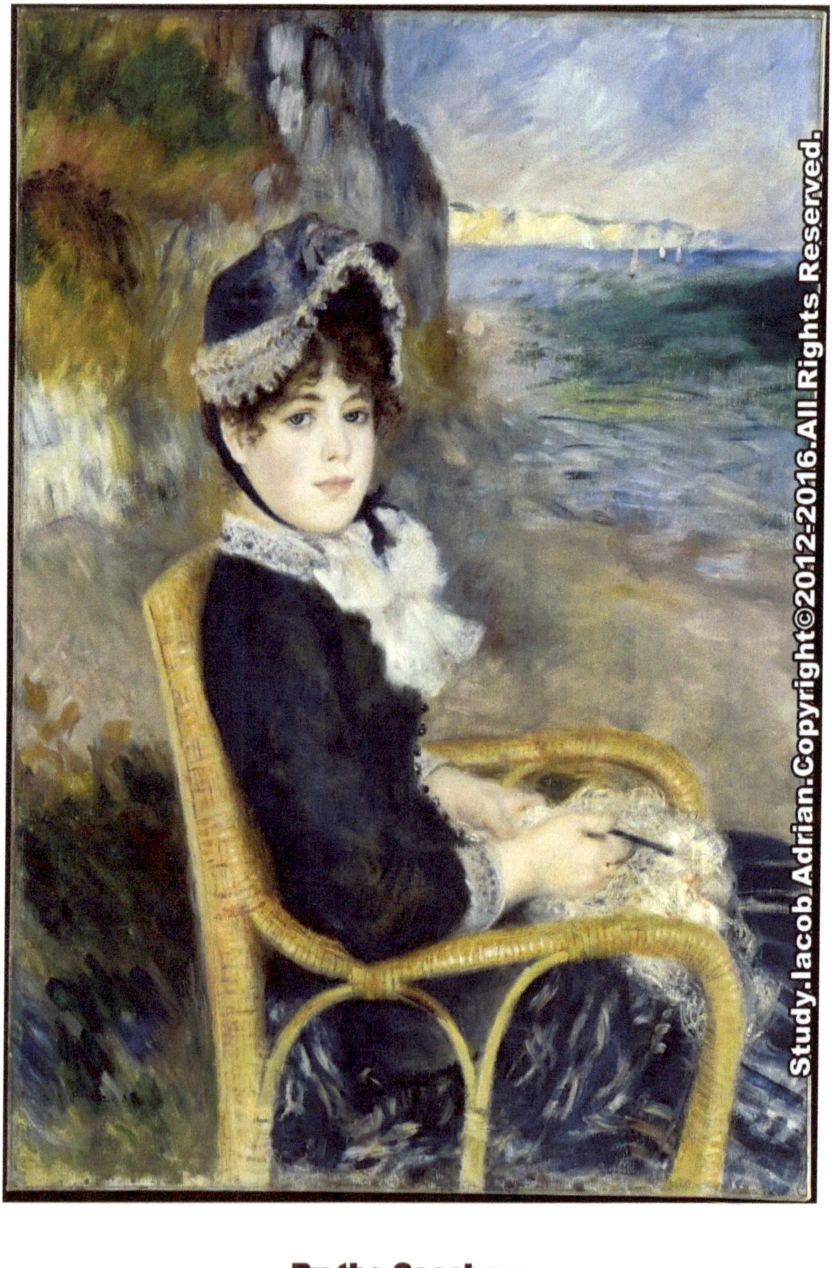

03

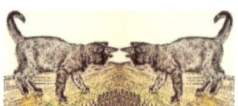

By the Seashore
Date : 1883

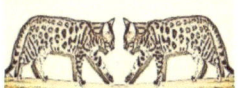

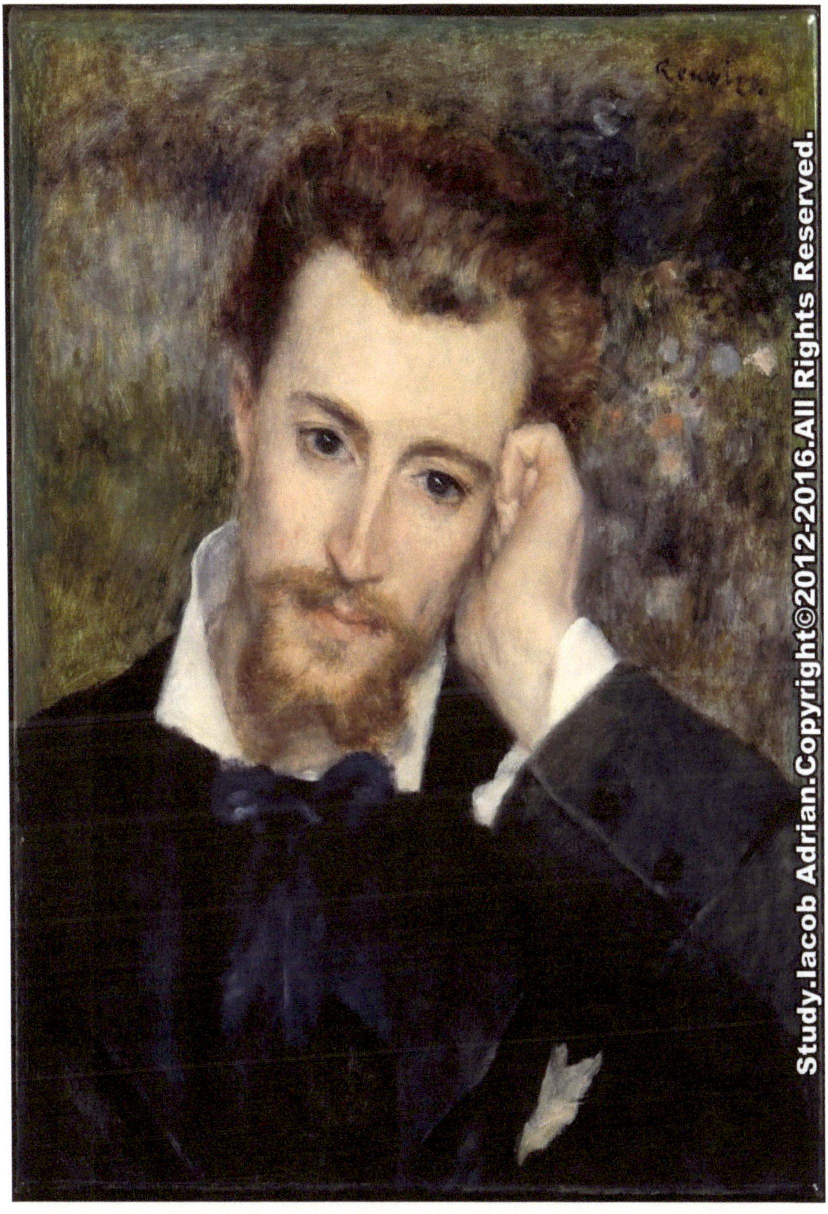

Eugène Murer (Hyacinthe-Eugène Meunier, 1841–1906)
Date : 1877

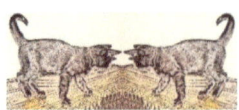

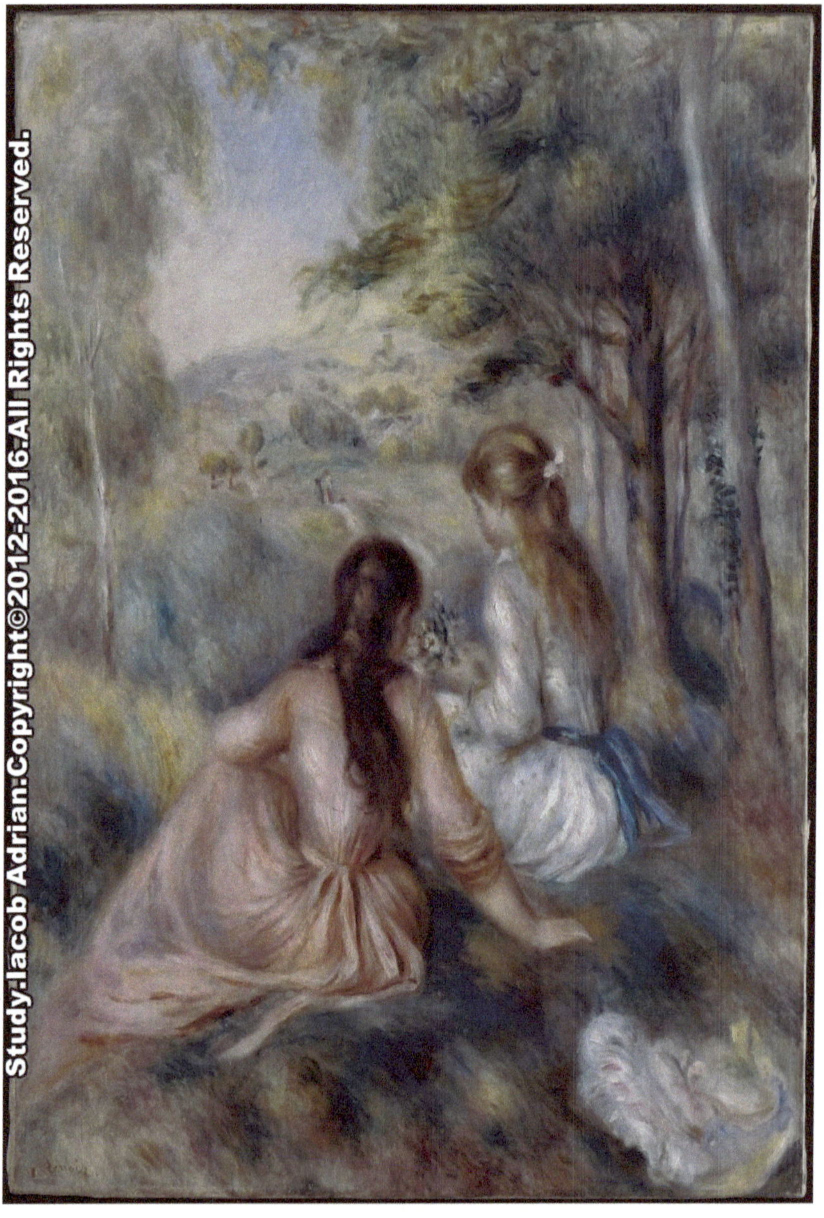

In the Meadow
Date : 1888–1892

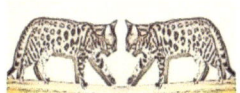

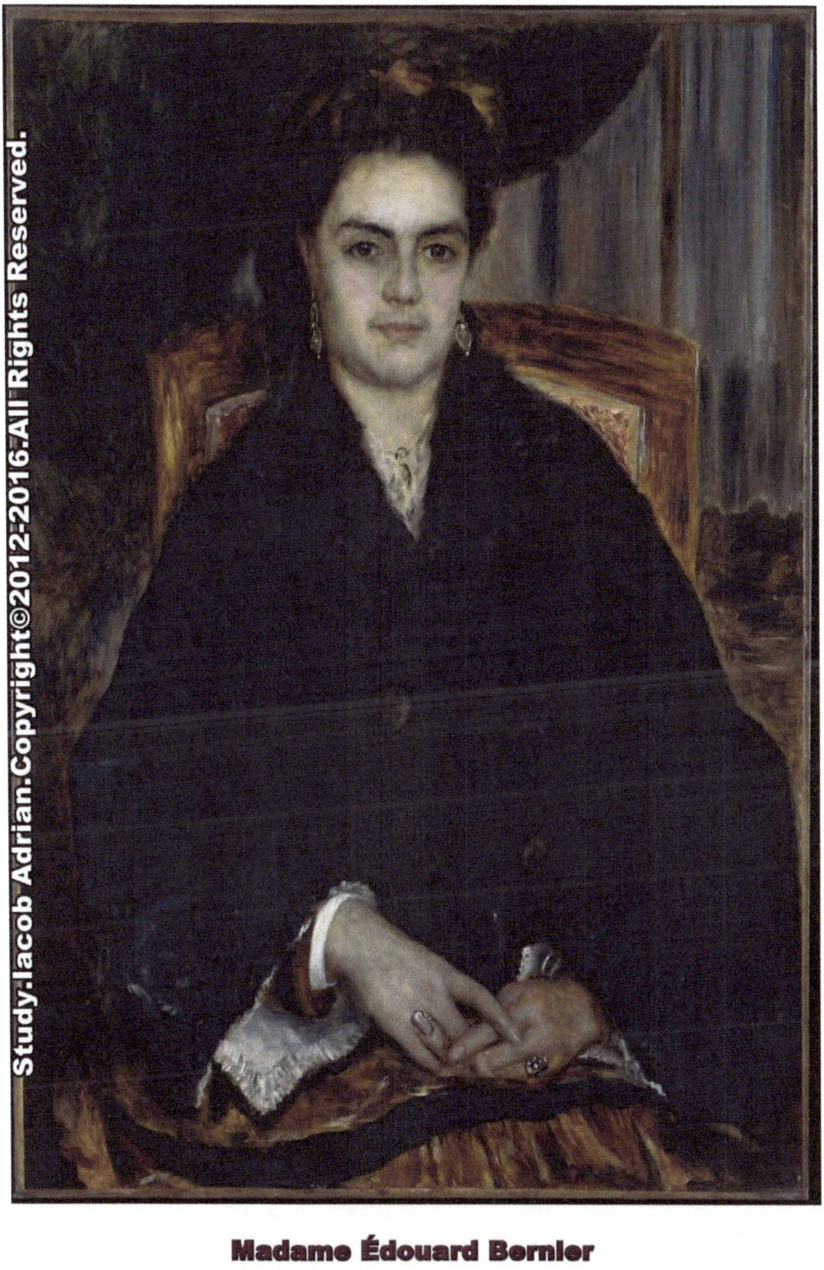

Madame Édouard Bernier
(Marie-Octavie-Stéphanie Laurens, 1838–1920)
Date : 1871

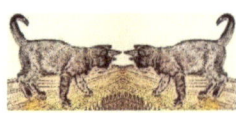

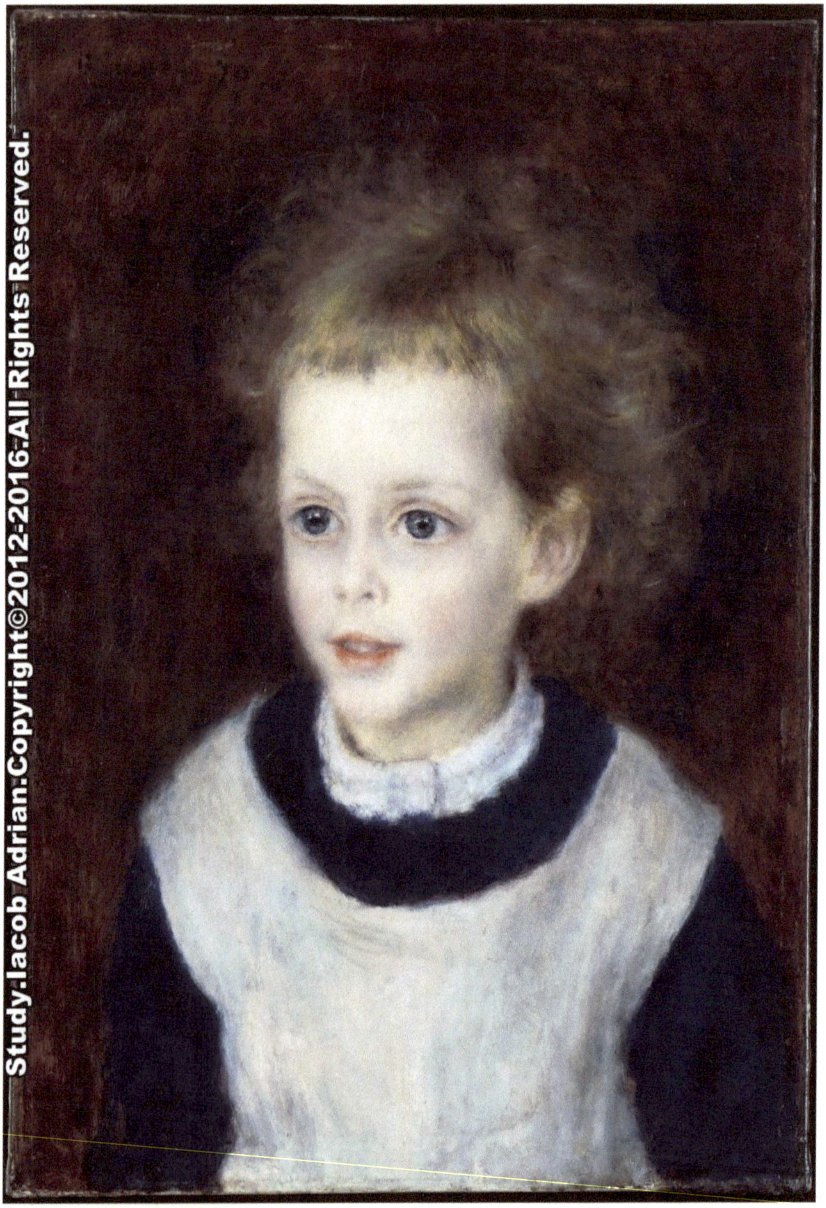

Marguerite-Thérèse (Margot) Berard (1874–1956)
Date : 1879

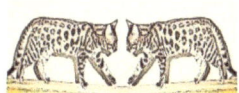

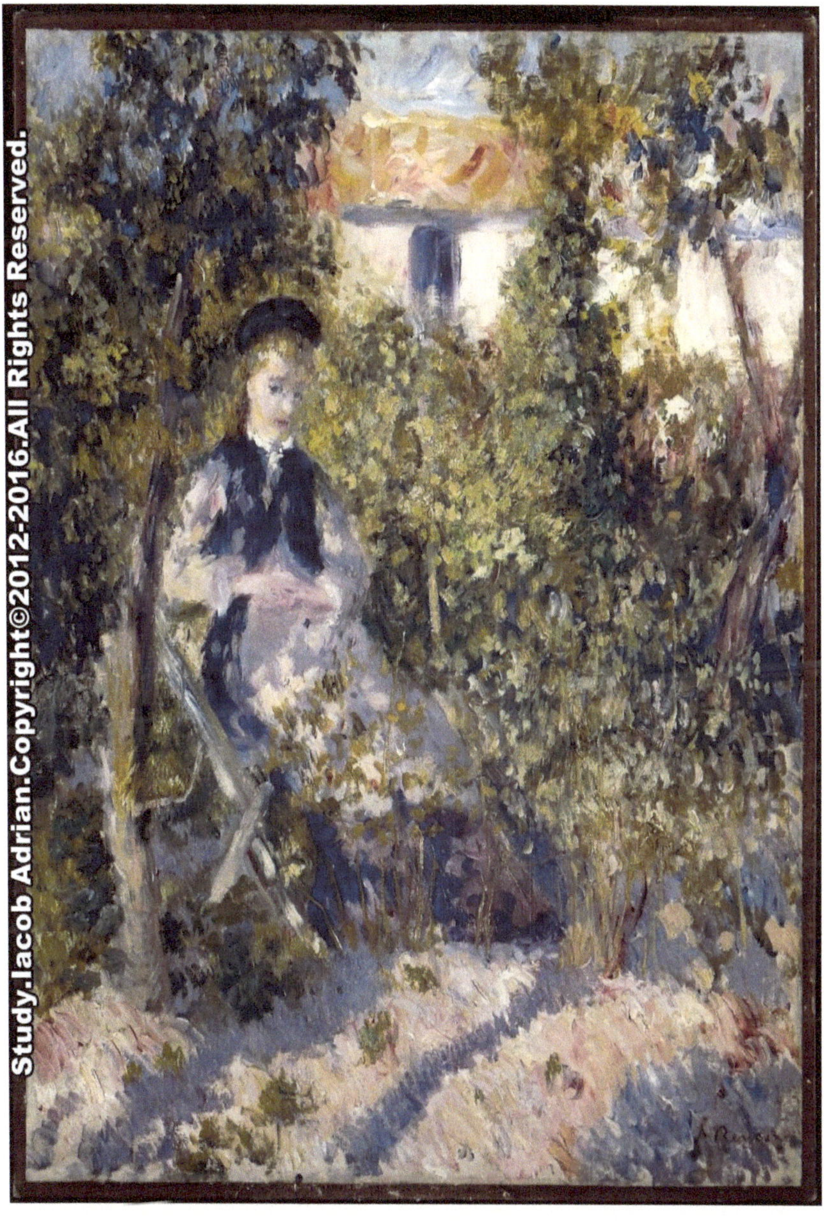

Nini in the Garden (Nini Lopez)
Date : 1876

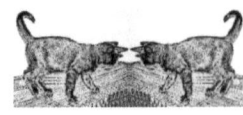

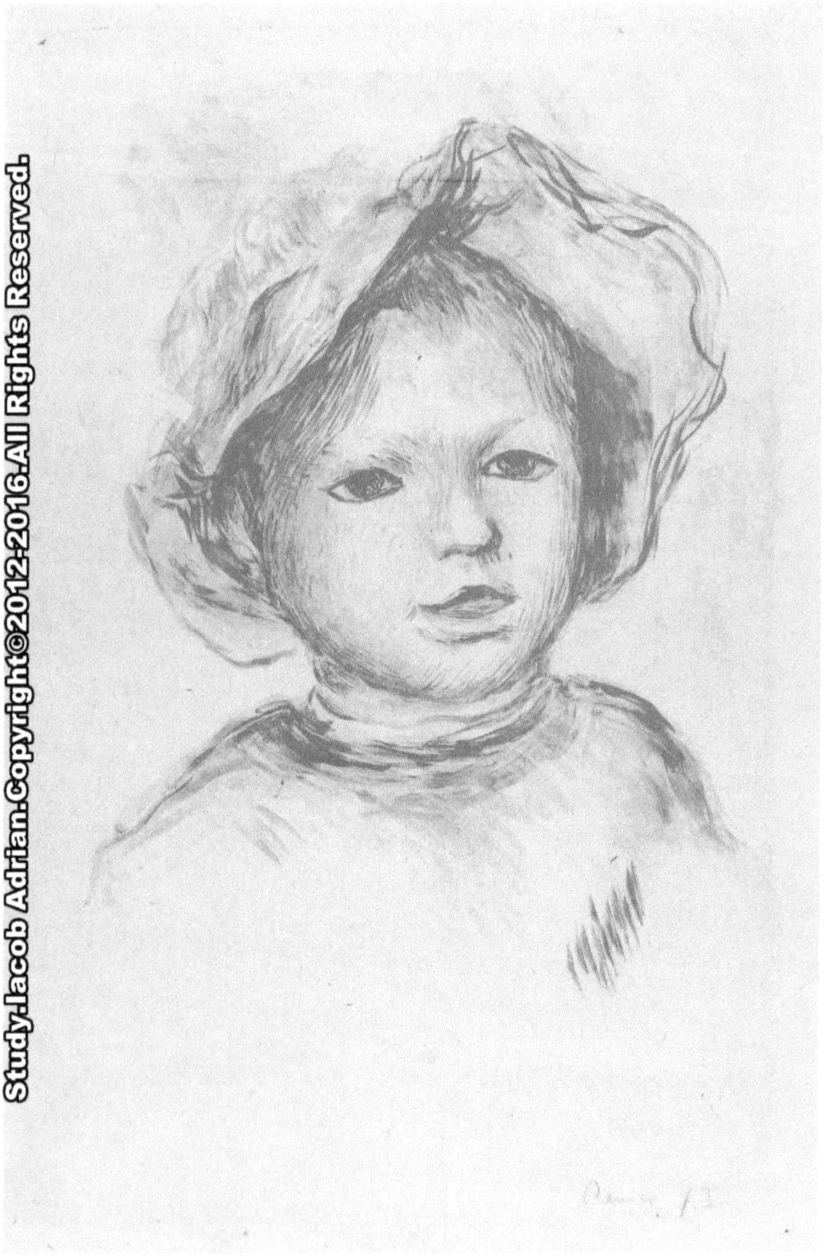

**Pierre Renoir from the Front
(Head of a Child / Tête d'enfant)
Date : 1893**

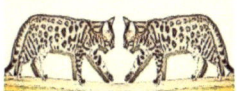

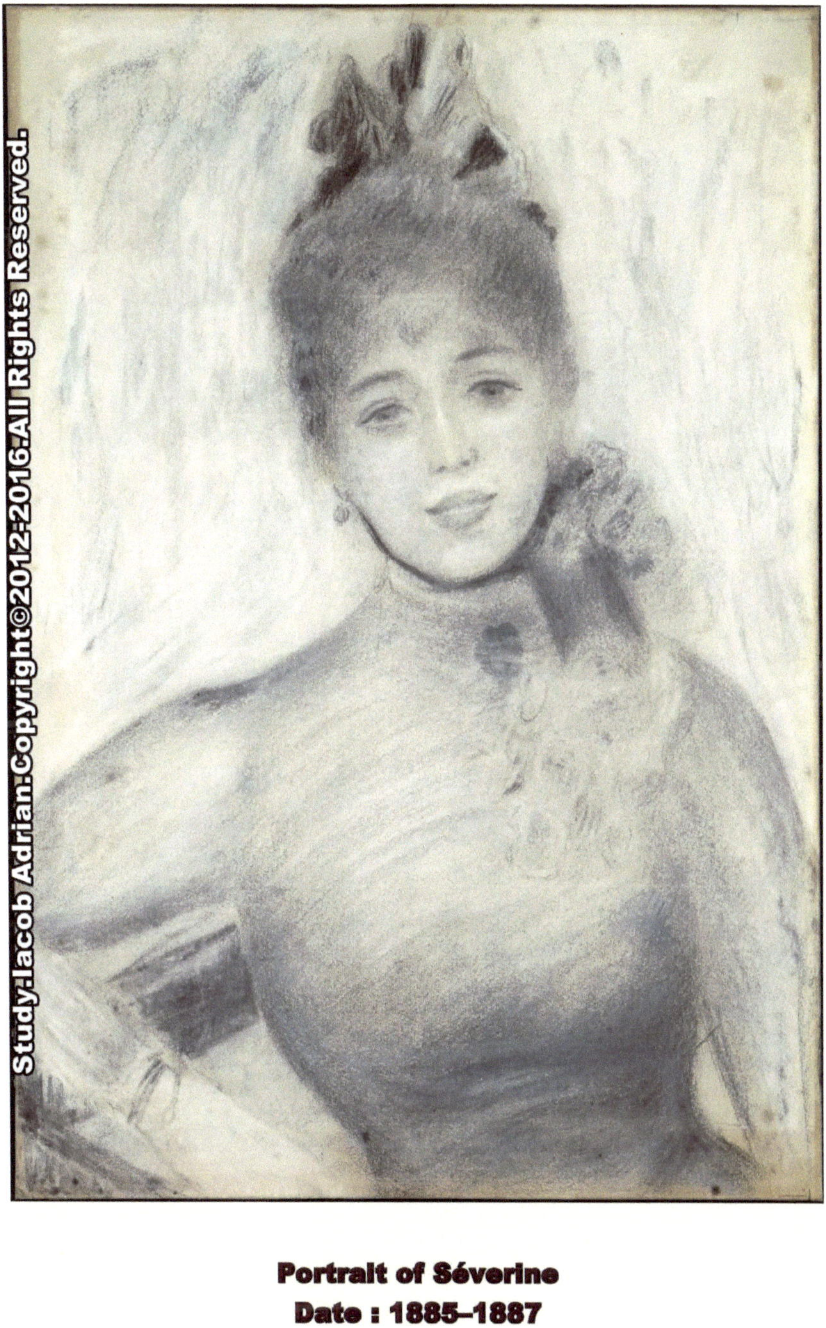

Portrait of Séverine
Date : 1885-1887

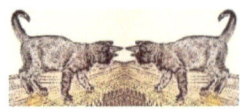

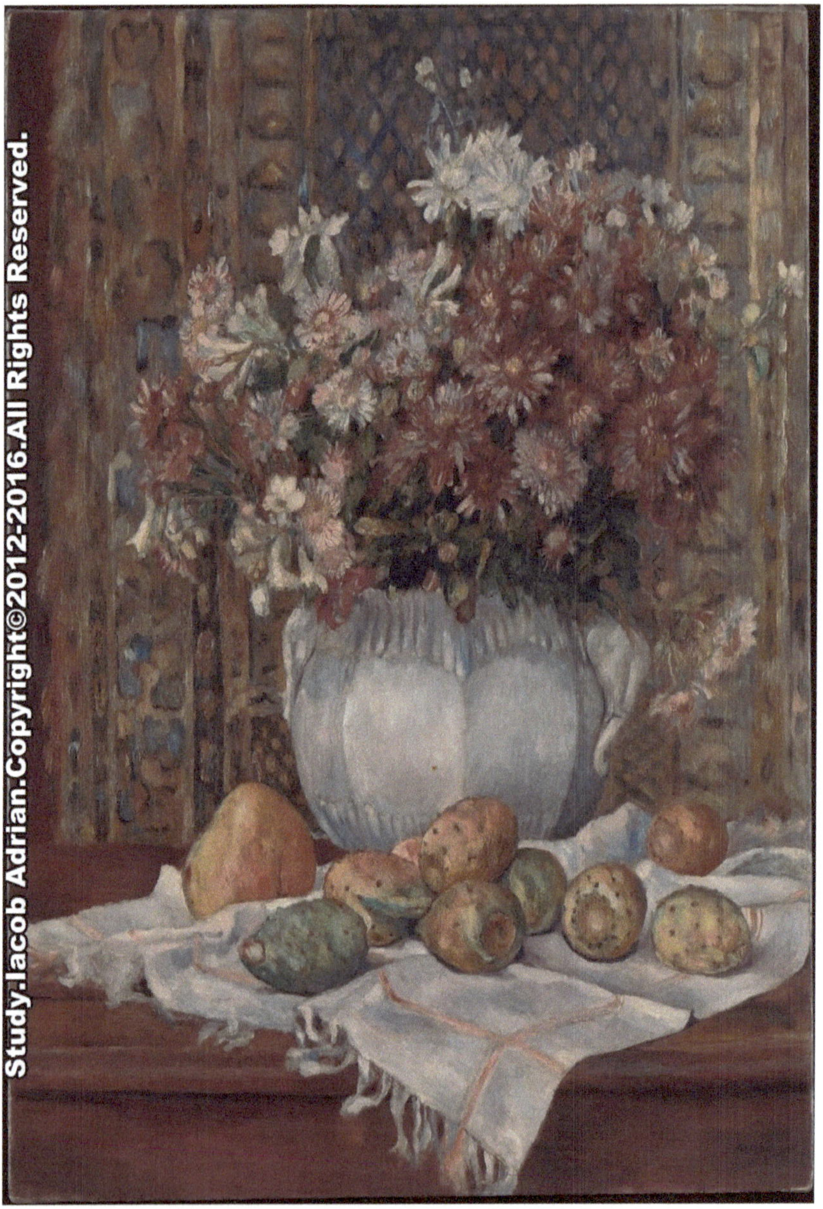

Still Life with Flowers and Prickly Pears
Date : circa 1885

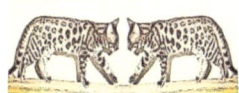

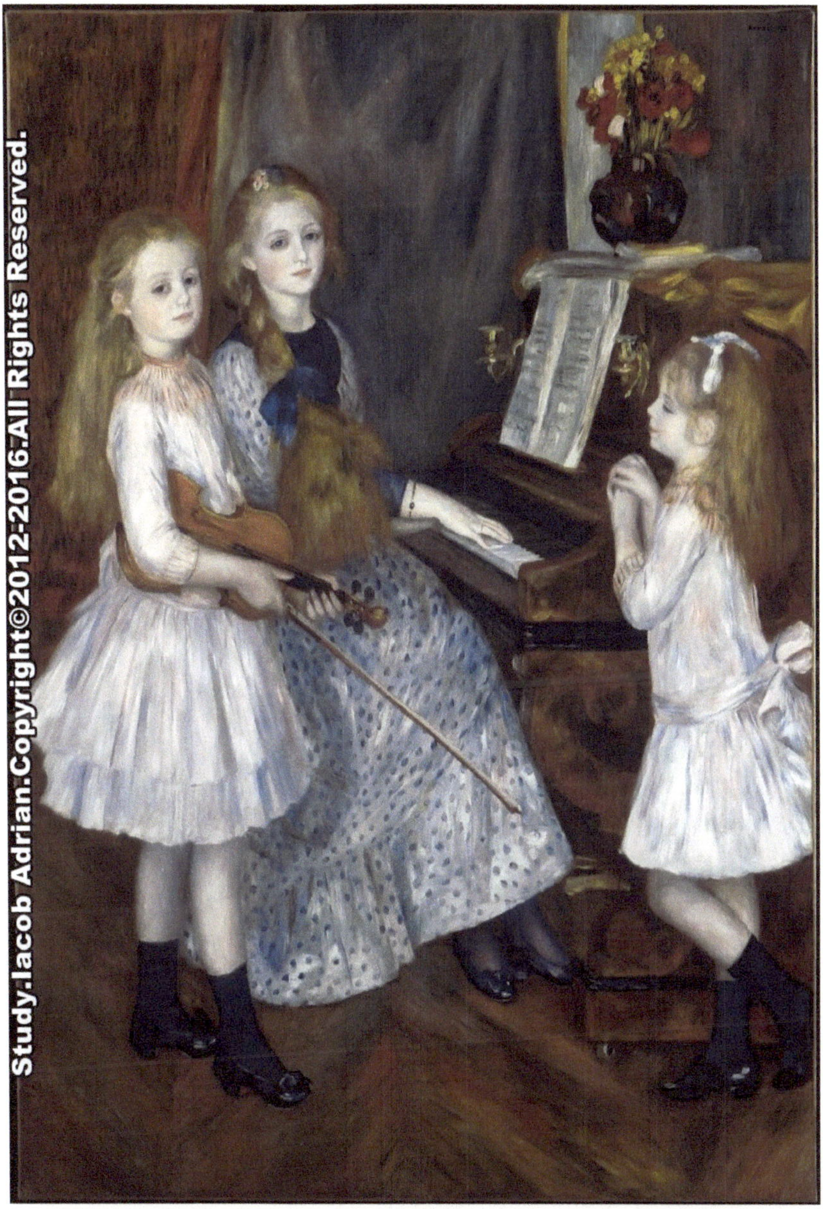

The Daughters of Catulle Mendès, Huguette (1871–1964), Claudine (1876–1937), and Helyonne (1879–1955)
Date : 1888

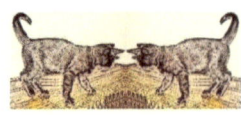

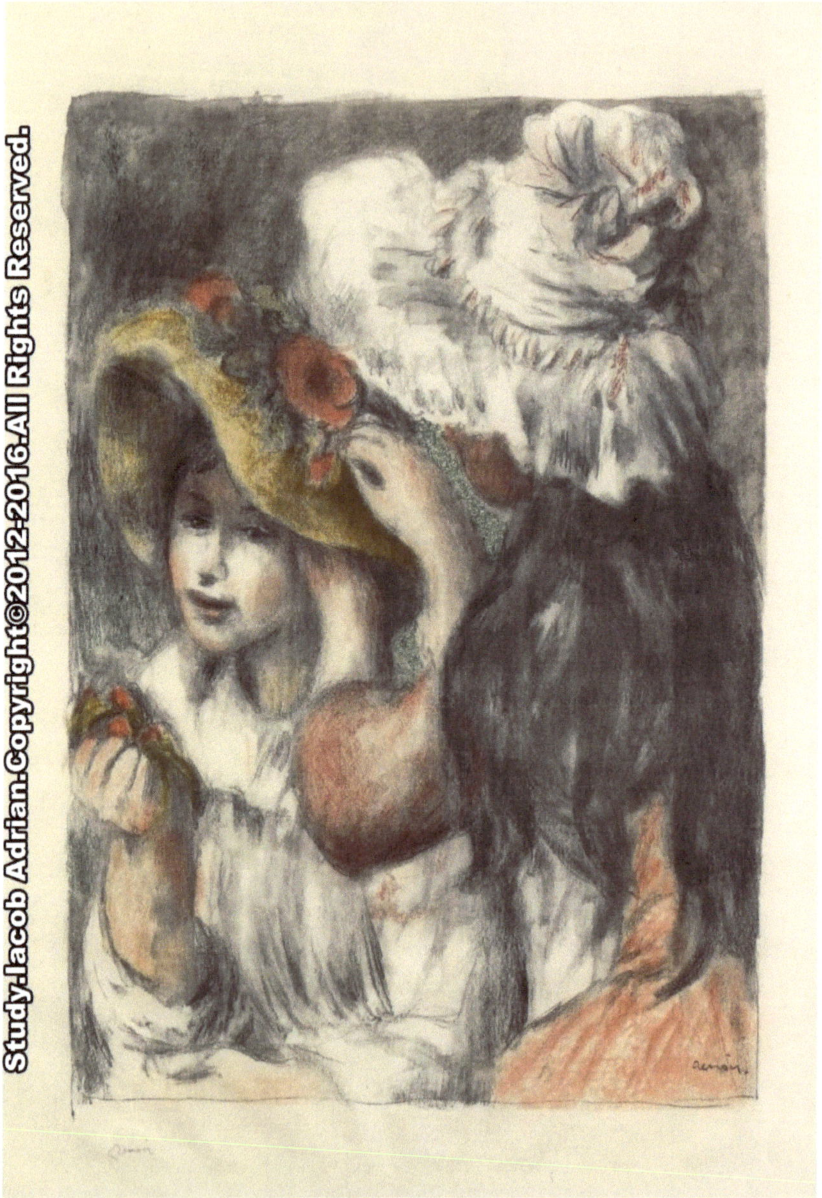

The Hat Pinned with Flowers (Le Chapeau Épinglé)
Date : 1898

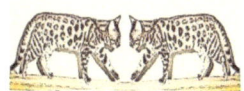

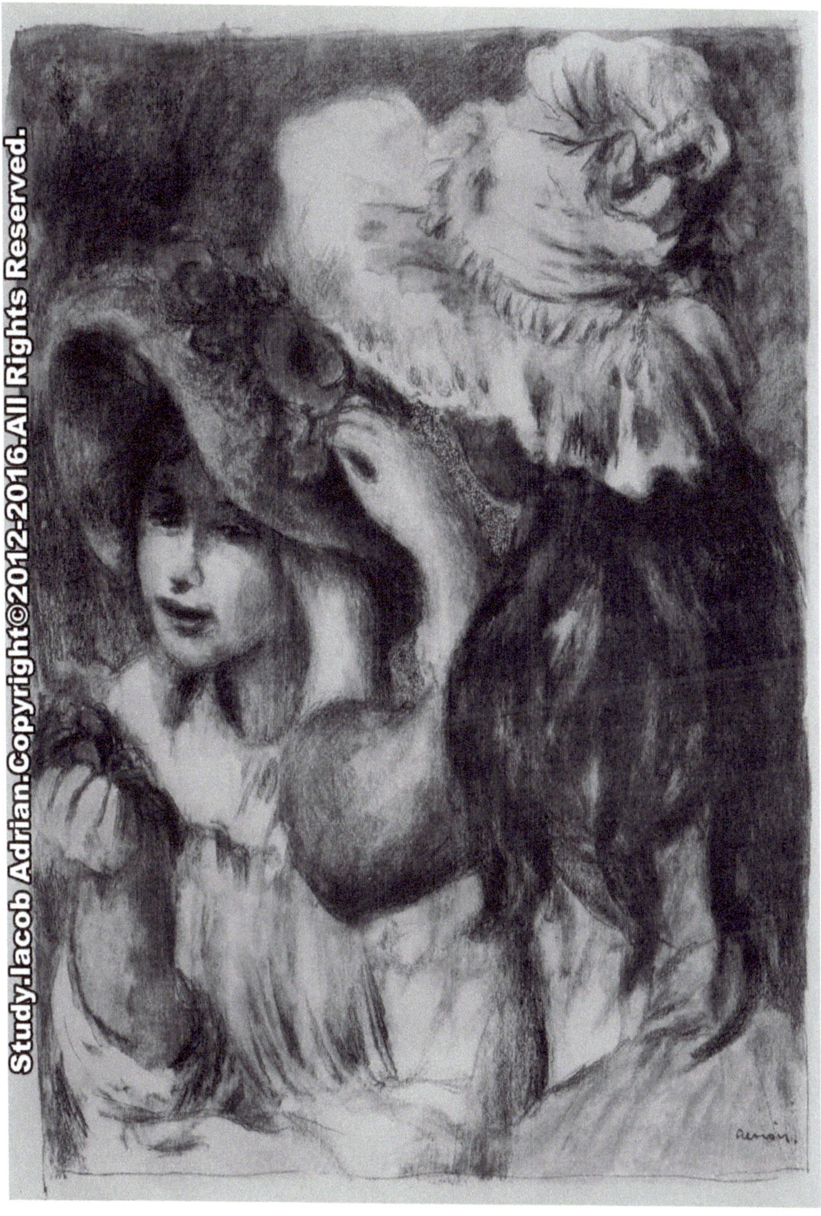

The Hat Pinned with Flowers (Le Chapeau Épinglé)
Date : 1898

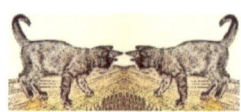

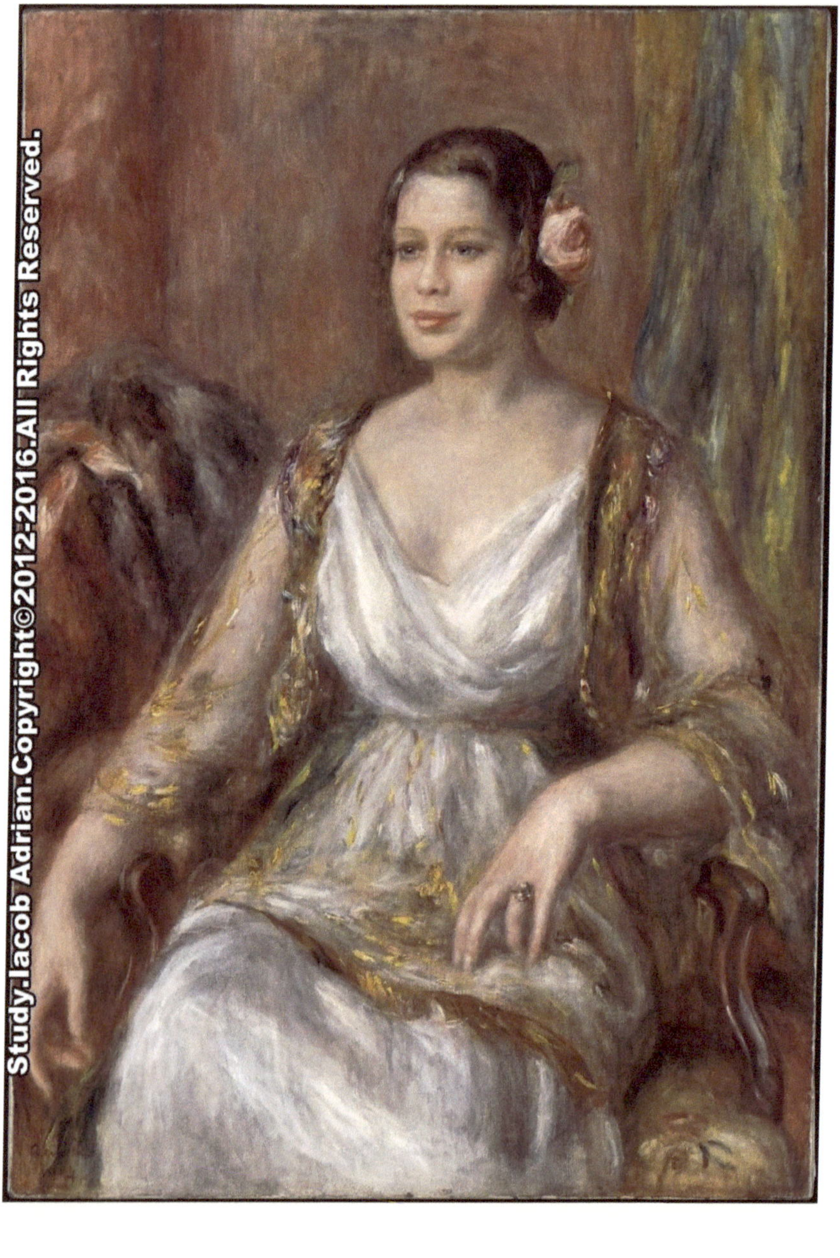

Tilla Durieux (Ottilie Godeffroy, 1880–1971)
Date : 1914

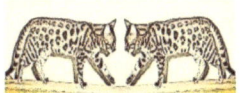

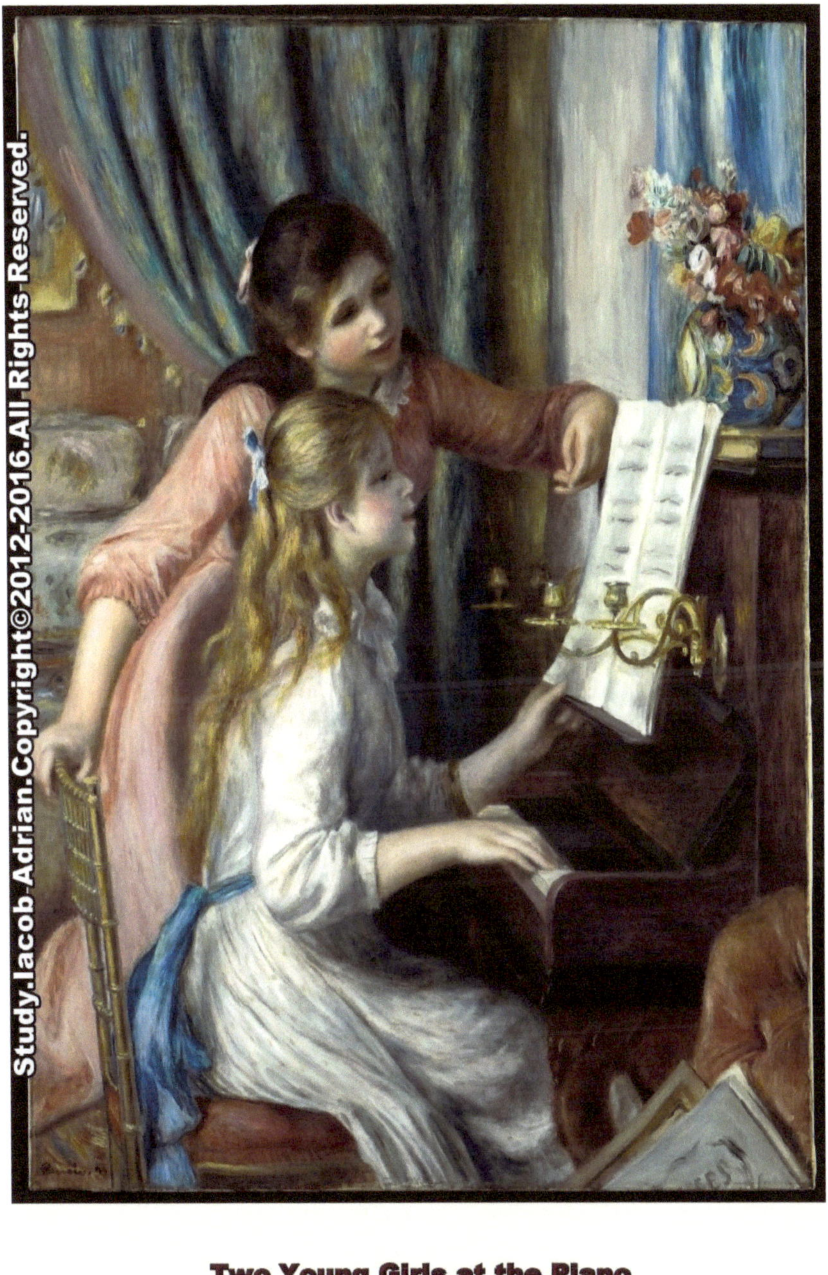

Two Young Girls at the Piano
Date : 1892

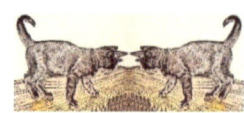

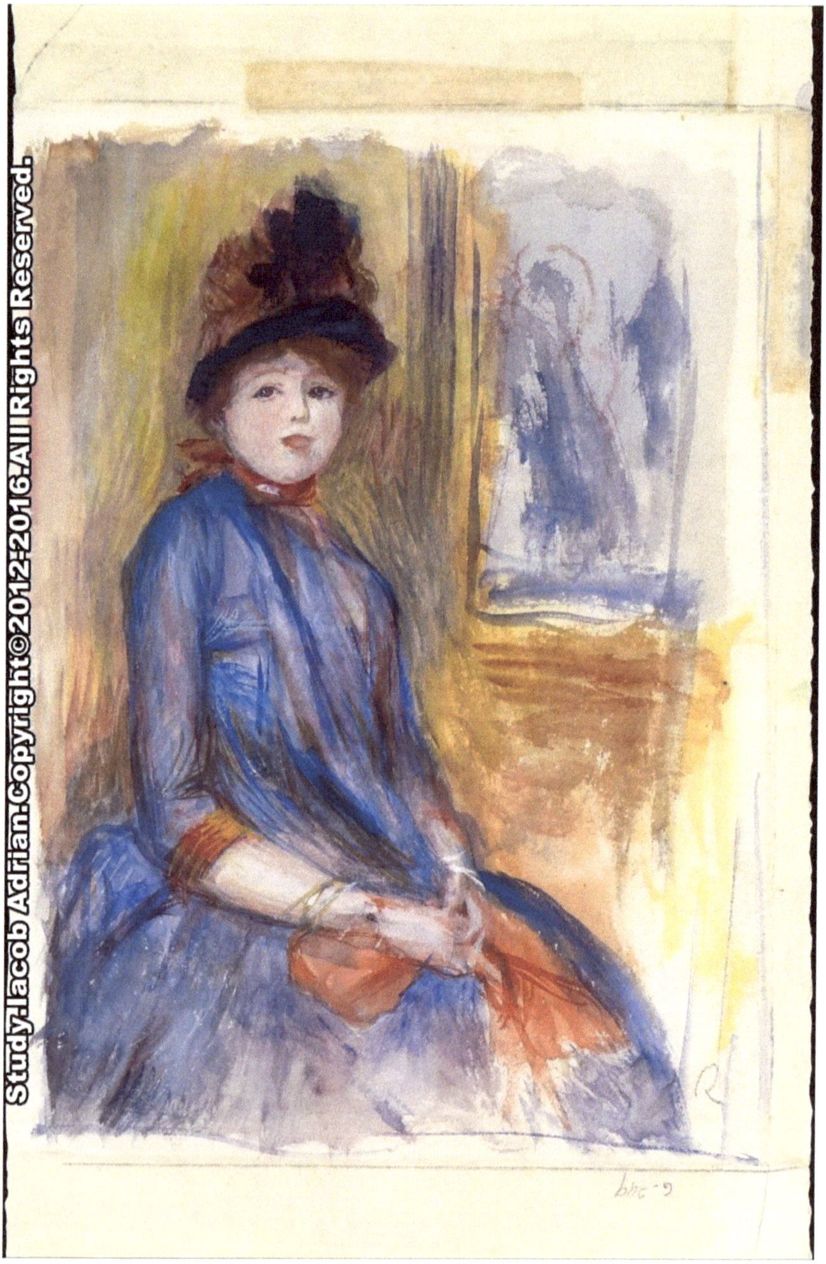

Young Girl in a Blue Dress
Date : ca. 1890

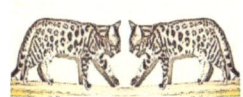

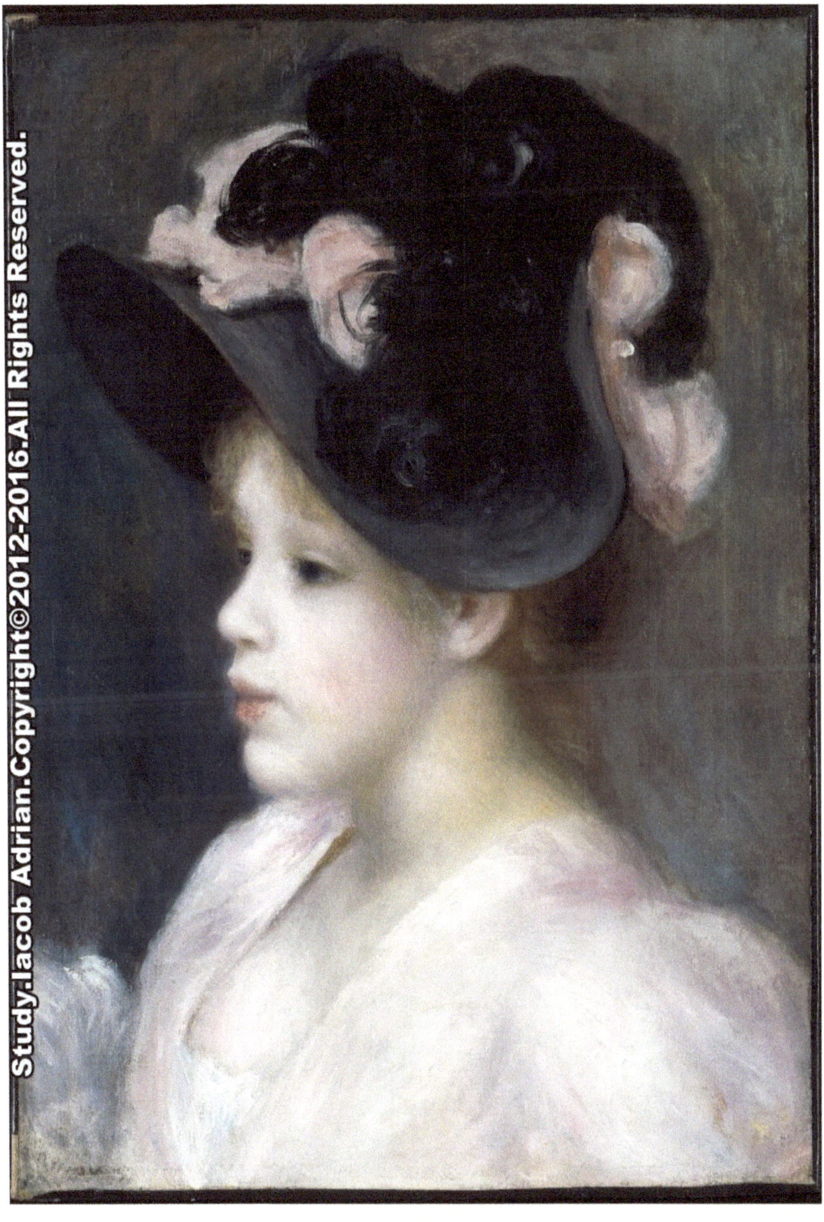

Young Girl in a Pink-and-Black Hat
Date : circa 1891

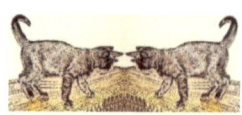

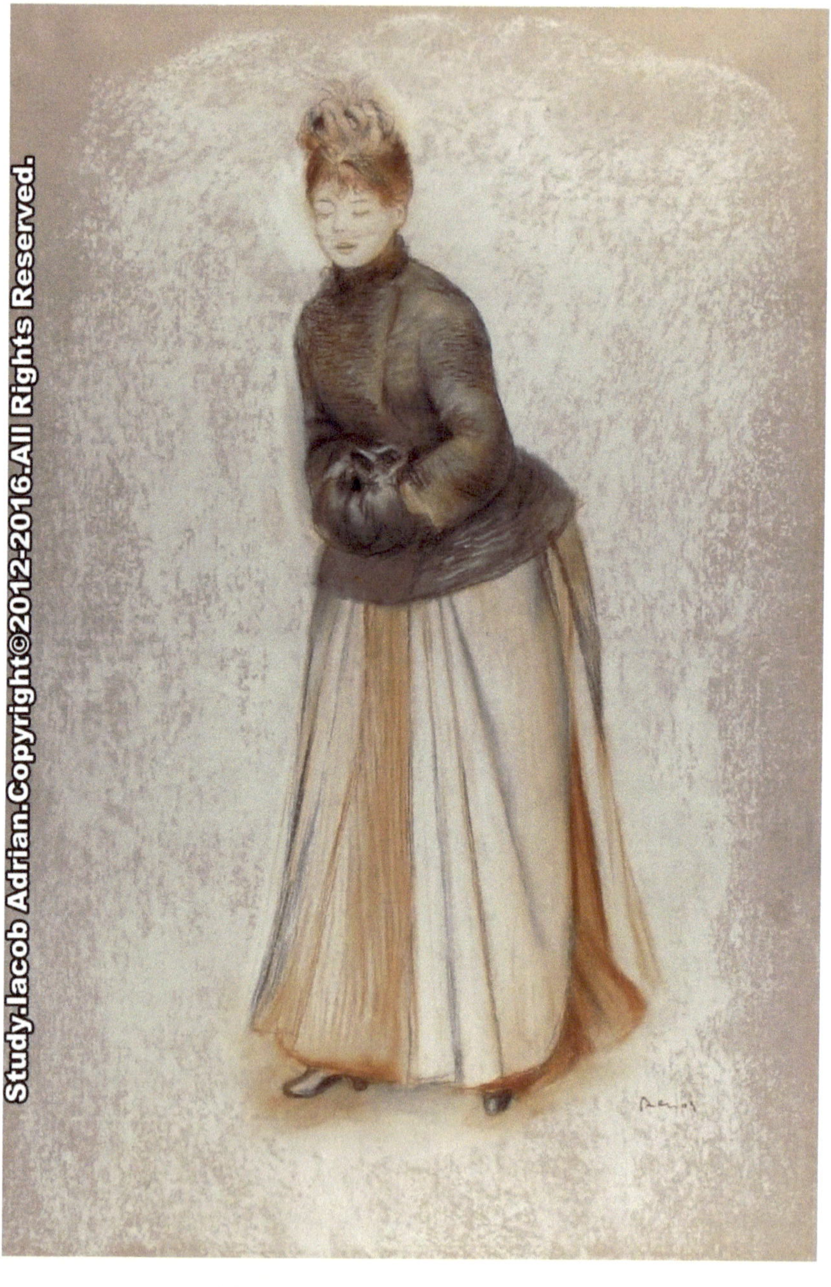

Young Woman with a Muff
Date : 1860–1919

Bibliographic sources :

**Based on Paintings of
Pierre-Auguste Renoir (1841-1919)**

and

Materials and/or elements from :
- Documentary Studies 1 collection,
- Documentary Studies 4 collection,
- Iacob Images K 4.0 collection,
Author / owner of collections : Iacob Adrian

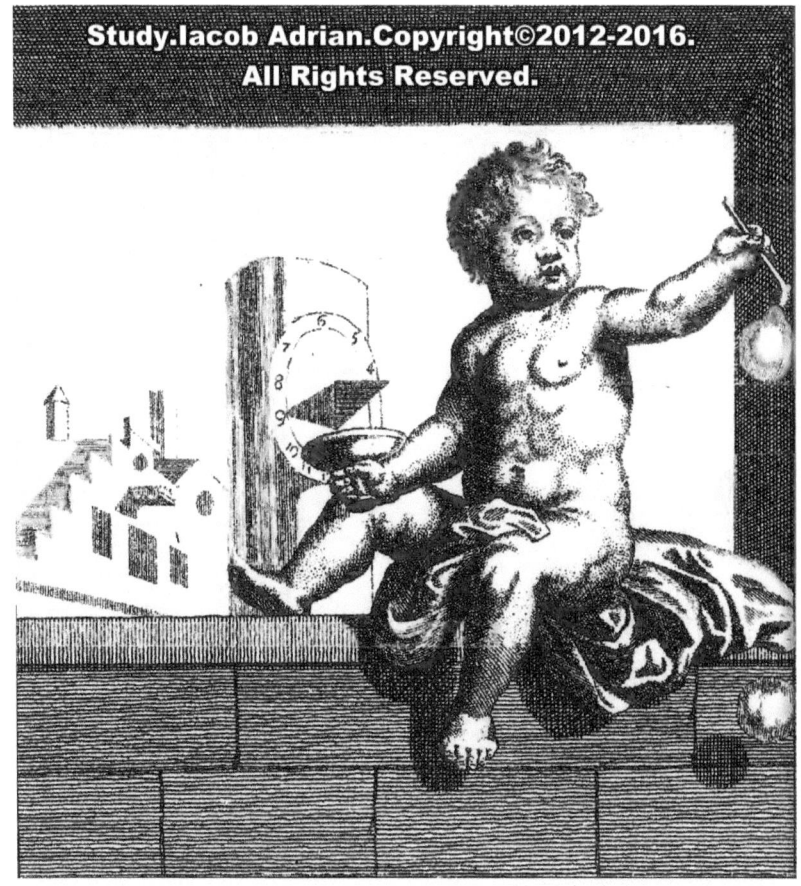

This documentary study use,
combined in various proportions,
elements from the following categories,
forms and subsets :
- fair use
- documentary
- documentary photography
- feature
- journalism
- arts journalism
- visual journalism
- photojournalism
- celebrity photography
in order to :
- employ material as the object of cultural critique ,
- quote to illustrate an argument or point ,
- use material in historical sequence,
providing independent opinion,
using photos, press articles, advertisements,
opinions of fans etc. ...

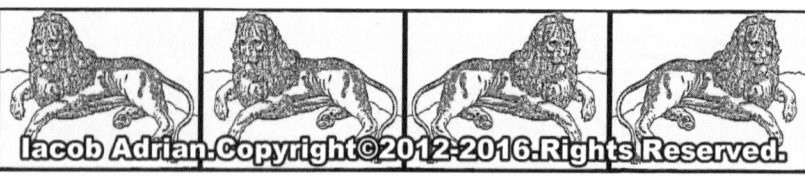

www.ingramcontent.com/pod-product-compliance
Lightning Source LLC
Chambersburg PA
CBHW040300220526
45473CB00002B/546